TOUCHED BY A CANYON

RAFTING THE GRAND CANYON DURING
COVID-19

Sue Hiser

Author's Tranquility Press
MARIETTA, GEORGIA

Copyright © 2022 by Sue Hiser

All rights reserved. No part of this publication may be reproduced, distributed or transmitted in any form or by any means, including photocopying, recording, or other electronic or mechanical methods, without the prior written permission of the publisher, except in the case of brief quotations embodied in critical reviews and certain other noncommercial uses permitted by copyright law. For permission requests, write to the publisher, addressed "Attention: Permissions Coordinator," at the address below.

Sue Hiser/Author's Tranquility Press
2706 Station Club Drive SW
Marietta, GA 30060
www.authorstranquilitypress.com

Ordering Information:
Quantity sales. Special discounts are available on quantity purchases by corporations, associations, and others. For details, contact the "Special Sales Department" at the address above.

Touched By a Canyon/ Sue Hiser
Paperback 978-1-959453-54-3
Ebook 978-1-959453-55-0

DEDICATION

Dedicated to healthcare workers for their competence, sacrifice, endurance and compassion as they carried us through COVID-19.

ACKNOWLEDGEMENTS

Accomplishments are more fun when experienced with others. Thank you to Ed for being patient with all of us until we had the courage to join him in the Grand Canyon. Thank you to my friends who had the courage to do this adventure. Thank you to my parents and siblings who supported me on this crazy adventure and all of the ones I've taken in my life. Thank you to my wife who lifts me every day of my life. Special thanks to my niece, Alex, whose expertise in design, editing, and consulting pushed me through the process of making this project a reality.

Table of Contents

Introduction 3
Travel In a Pandemic 7
Heat 15
W.O.W: Wall of Water 21
CAMPING 101 29
Vacation chores 29
Coffee & Laughter 44
"Hey you guys …!" 52
Who Do You Take on Vacation? 58
Why We Do What We Do 64
Passion and synchronicity 75
What Awakens You? 83
Endings 89
ABOUT THE AUTHOR 95

Introduction

Keep the Magic Alive

My goal with a vacation is to keep the wonderful feeling of rest, excitement and connection alive at least until the following Wednesday. You know how it is, as soon as you return to work or to the real world you get hit by a barrage of emails, fires that have gone on, drama that people want to catch you up on. It's all the stuff that was irrelevant to you while you were on vacation and is now high priority. I've even said to my team at one point, "Your job is to make my first day back sane." I have a friend who stays home on the Monday after vacation just so she can catch up on email and make the reentry into the world of work a little easier.

The white-water rafting trip to the Grand Canyon was definitely different. The wonder of being in the Grand Canyon stayed with me in ways that I haven't had a vacation stay with me. Maybe it was influenced by the fact we traveled there in August 2020 in the midst of COVID-19. Maybe it was returning, continuing to sequester and working from home but for some reason the feeling of wonder did not leave me. We returned on Wednesday to

Ohio, the day after we got off the river. I took off the rest of the week and perhaps that additional time was a factor. I woke up at two or three in the morning and would reach for my pen because the thoughts coming to me needed written down. The memories from being in the canyon stayed with me and I sought out information and books to round out the story, and to continue the connection.

The one trip guide gave me a book about the experiences of the river guides. I read the chapters as if they were a smooth chocolate to savor – slowly, mindfully. I read a chapter; put the book down and walk away to reflect. I didn't want the book to end. When it did end, I found the list of the different writers and their websites. I followed each path of discovery on the websites fascinated by their stories and their lives. I checked the internet for other pictures, videos, and even other rafting groups. I checked Amazon for books, and then reserved them at the library, and waited eagerly for the emails that would tell me the books had arrived to be picked up using the safe, socially distanced protocol. Libraries closed to the public in 2020– the madness of it all.

Nearly every day I scrolled through the pictures on my phone that I had taken. I reviewed the photo books from the library. I read through the essays of other peoples' experiences rafting through the canyon. I couldn't get enough. I even bought an adult coloring book of the canyon and studied the real pictures to try to duplicate it with colored pencils. (BTW – coloring is a great coping mechanism for political turmoil that was also present when I returned.) There was something about the simplicity of being in nature but the complexity of the depths of the canyon and the water that seemed to open me up. The short essays that follow are those pieces that needed written otherwise they wouldn't let me go, and I would not sleep.

Everyone should raft down the Grand Canyon, but can everyone? No – and there's a lot of reasons for not being able to do so. Was the trip on my bucket list? Uh, no. How I even ended up there is a bit of a surprise especially during COVID-19 and now as I reflect on that happenstance – was I really invited to the Grand Canyon, or had I been summoned? There is a difference.

Join me for a short time to experience the river, the sand, the heat – THE Grand Canyon from the safety of your own home.

Travel In a Pandemic

Questions & Answers

If you had the chance to vacation in a state with high COVID-19 cases would you do it, or stay home? Would you go if you knew you were going to be living around strangers for eight days and seven nights? What would stop you? What would push you forward?

The idea of the trip began nearly two years earlier by a friend, Ed, who rafted through the Grand Canyon in 2010. For years he talked about his incredible experience and for a number of years we listened and said, "Good for you!"

My wife, Chelsea, and I could see the experience changed him and was a great launch to his early retirement. Yet, we had no intention of going and no desire to pee in a river in front of friends and strangers, use a toilet and change clothes in the wide open, and then navigate the Colorado River white water rapids the highest ranked ones overall. I'm not sure when our minds changed and became open to the possibility.

Initially the answer was 'Oh hell no!" to the question 'Are you the type of person who will sleep outdoors, and be away from civilization?" That wasn't who we were, or were we? Old friends said they would love to do the trip and opened our eyes to the possibility that maybe we were those kinds of people. Peer pressure is alive and well even after 25 plus years of friendship and we hated to miss out on a trip if college friends saw themselves as river rafters. We asked the early retiree to let us know if he ever decided to do the trip again. Fast forward to 2018 and the call came. Shortly thereafter, friends who escaped a hurricane on the east coast stayed with us for a few days and we posed the idea of a Grand Canyon rafting trip. Over the next few days we looked at online videos of rafting trips in the Canyon. It looked scary and awesome at the same time. "Would you do it?" we asked each other and soon we had ten of us committed and paying for the trip. 2020 began with the excitement that we would be on the Colorado River in August. Then COVID-19 arrived.

Six of us connected via a Friday night zoom call. We are college friends from the 80's and initially this call was a way to touch base and to stay sane in the midst of COVID-19. One Friday night led to another Friday night and then another. We caught up about COVID-19 since two of us are in healthcare while another is in education. COVID-19 became more real when there were deaths in the nursing home where one is an administrator. I was coaching leaders within our hospitals and hearing of their challenges with their teams as they managed through the earlier ambiguity of COVID-19. It was April and periodically we wondered about our August white water rafting trip but that was far into the future and potentially life would return to the new normal by then.

Throughout May and into June all river trips in the Grand Canyon were canceled. Then we received notice of a phased reopening of the Colorado River beginning June 14. Our trip was on! But there were many questions and challenges. COVID-19 cases increased in Arizona and Nevada. Ohio cases did not dwindle as planned and Memorial Weekend brought an uptick in cases. Yet the idea of a vacation on the horizon changed the Friday night phone calls and it felt as if a fresh spring breeze had entered the house. Suddenly there were traveling and hiking clothes to find or buy, packing lists to review, and bags to find.

Zoom calls began to be reveal parties as we shared the new things that had been shipped to us or new items we bought. Bags were revealed for the size that we were taking to hold all of our stuff.

Funny how much faith you place into a travel company. My comrades were content to go with whatever the travel company said, but I had more questions. I didn't want to live my life by fear and I hated to miss out on a trip of a lifetime, but just saying a blind 'yes' wasn't setting with me. I had concerns which I expressed to my wife. She saw the perspective of our colleagues but supported me with all of my doubts and questions. I didn't want to miss out, but I had a lot of concerns. Instead of the questions that started with 'what about ... ' and then ended with something that the rafting company hadn't addressed, I started to ask myself a different question, "How could I feel safe in this situation?"

Trips were beginning in June so we'd have a chance to learn from them. I planned to call the travel group in late June and throughout July to discover if there were any problems with the first few trips. I would become a pain, but that's what healthy people do who want to stay healthy. Plus I monitored the numbers of COVID-19 cases down to the counties where the trip was based.

My first phone call asked the rafting staff what they were doing to ensure safety with the pandemic. They shared their new practices of: reducing the number of people on the trip, conducting pre-screenings, requiring a mask around food, increasing sanitizing between trips and taking peoples' temperatures every single day. Good to know.

My next call was to the hotel where we would stay a few days before the trip. They had reduced occupancy to 30%, instituted social distancing, sanitized on a regular basis, limited people allowed in the pool and closed the fitness center. These were all good things to know. The HVAC people never returned my call (okay – maybe THAT was too much) but I was curious about the filtering system in the hotel rooms.

The second phone call back to the river company was to find out what they would do if somebody had a fever? What were the options? You are in the middle of a canyon and no medical services in sight. Where would they take you? When I posed that question to the Friday night group they laughed at me and said the rafting company was now creating the manual based on my phone calls. I didn't care. The rafting company had a response, even though it was untested to date (good to know). The first step was isolation and the second step was emergency evacuation which begged the question to what hospitals because based on cases you didn't want to go to Phoenix. They agreed that Flagstaff was better.

I knew hospitals were preparing ethical guidelines for staff to follow on who should get treatment if hospitals were in overflow and medicine for the virus was limited. As my friends laughed at me – I pointed out that we might not be high on the list of priorities in another city. They did not care!

Between phone calls I talked to people at work. We were required to take time-off in order to burn vacation time and improve self-care, but where could you go? Before or after meetings people shared what they were doing with their time-off and the different plans that had fallen through for them. When I shared that our trip was on the response of whether they would do it or not was mixed. More people than I anticipated said emphatically, "Yes, I'd do it if I could!" There was one person's opinion I really wanted to know, but I also didn't want to know their response. I almost didn't tell him, but when I did I wasn't surprised when he said he would NOT do the trip. I respect this person's opinion a great deal – his knowledge of COVID-19 was almost scary. The fact I did the trip after his comment is probably more attributed to FOMO, 'fear of missing out' with my friends than anything. I did not want to live my life in fear, a comment reinforced by my 87 year old mother which is a high endorsement on the fear scale.

Final check was flying. Planes were also a scary part of the entire process. How could you feel safe on a plane especially when Dr. Anthony Fauci, Chief Medical Advisor to the President, was saying he wouldn't go on a plane now at all. I'm sure the airlines requested clarification by him of opting not to fly due to his age – he's over 70. But we had a 70 year old in our group. I found out later there were a number of our fellow rafters from the west coast who drove to Las Vegas versus being on a plane. Because our entire group was either Midwest or East Coast, we all flew. I finally added a face shield along with the mask. Yes, I looked ridiculous but I was comforted by the fact that a lot of people who worked for the Airport and TSA were also wearing face shields. Since then, I've seen a recommendation for people to wear face shields when they fly.

I had a strategy. I asked a lot of questions. But, the most important question had been the one I posed to myself, "What do I need to do to feel safe?" We live in interesting times. If you feel fear or you don't feel safe – what stops you, what pulls you forward? The questions we ask reveal even more than answers. The path forward and adventure is uncovered. Whew, so much to do just to get to the trip.

Reading about travel prompts you to think of your own adventures. At the end of each chapter answer the questions provided.

You have the chance to vacation with friends but the activities are risky and outside your comfort zone. What would stop you? What would push you forward?

Heat

What comforts are you willing to leave ...

Heat! Hot! Oppressive heat was the weather that greeted us when we stepped out of the airport and waited for our Uber to arrive. The pavement didn't help but we also were in the parking garage so not in direct sun. The air was stifling and the reprieve of an air-conditioned car was eagerly awaited, but also a reminder that we would not be in air conditioning soon.

At home I sleep in 68° temperatures with two fans moving air in the bedroom. What had I signed up for? Average temperatures in the canyon in August were 103° in the day and a low of 75° at night. But the floor of the canyon would reach 120°. Gulp.

Ed, the crazy early retiree friend who we would blame if this all went south, kept saying not to worry because the river was right there so it would be easy to cool off. I had visions of sleeping in the river and waking up shriveled up like a prune like I was as a kid when I refused to get out of the pool despite chattering teeth and nearly uncontrolled shivering.

Our friends were already at the hotel. We greeted each other with masks on, quick hugs that we wanted to disappear into but knew we couldn't. We had a suite in the hotel which gave us room to separate as well as a common area with a kitchen. I calculated that if we picked up the virus in the airport or in the hotel we would start to show symptoms on Thursday of the trip at the earliest. I tried to keep my distance within the hotel but it wasn't easy.

We spent our few days in Las Vegas poolside, walking a little, but otherwise sequestered. Time at the hotel pool was done in blocks that we had to register for and then the area would be cleared and thoroughly cleaned. This was definitely not the experience we planned when we scheduled the trip but we adjusted just as we had been doing since March.

We arrived Saturday and would leave at 3:30 AM for the other hotel on Tuesday morning. There we would pick up a bus and travel with the entire group for five hours and arrive at Lees Ferry to load the rafts and takeoff. I savored the sheets and the pillows of the hotel bed really enjoying the crisp white feel and allowing all the senses of my body to drink them in. "Enjoy it while you can." I told Chelsea.

Chelsea was getting quieter the closer we got to departure but quiet at 3:30 in the morning is easy to chalk up to disrupted sleep. On the bus I checked on her after we had both napped for a bit. "You OK?"

"Yeah" she said but it was a stoic response not her normal "Yes of course" I had checked on her a couple times in that manner since March and her response always started with her sweeping her arms across the room in front of her, "I'm retired -it's all good!" This is the wonder of retiring very young due to working in public service.

"The fun of the trip is kind of over for you, isn't it? "I said quietly with a little teasing in my voice but it was the tease of knowing this woman for over 30 years and knowing what makes her happy. "You've done all the shopping and preparing and now there's nothing left to do."

"Yeah," She smiled a little sheepishly that I had called out her truth. She wasn't the only one like this on the trip. Others later admitted the amount of fun they had shopping, especially on Amazon, to secure all their gear.

Chelsea loves to travel and a big part of that love is the complexity of preparing, planning and the discovery of the best deal. The best deal means cheapest and best value with best discount. If there's more time to investigate, she can get an even better deal. She can find the right combination of shoes, sandals, jackets, shirt, flashlight, cleaning supplies and under clothes. Nothing missed scrutiny. In the last 8 to 10 weeks I walked out of my home office to another bunch of shopping bags to review contents and help make decisions.

I knew better than to buy into one idea too much because the next day could have a better find. Thank goodness she was adept at also returning things as the next new thing replaced yesterday's purchase. For example we had five bags to choose from as to which bag we would take to carry our things. The dimensions had to be no bigger than 12x12x24 - we had three that might work and two new ones that had been purchased. All the new ones were returned and Chelsea used one that she's had for well over ten years.

I shudder to think of the money wasted and the stuff piled in the corners of our house if she was not equally effective at returning rejected items. The people at the Eddie Bauer warehouse knew her very well.

I reaped the benefits of her expertise. I had brand new water sandals and a camp sandal that was a plastic version of my favorite leather shoe that we found years earlier on vacation but had not been able to replace. I didn't need many new clothes and ended up using some of her older clothes. Chelsea insisted she didn't need anything new either for clothes - after all - it was going to be two outfits worn for multiple days but soon new T-shirts were justified.

"Look they're so cute and I got a great deal!"

She looked awesome on the trip, but as we drove five hours toward Lake Powell and Lees Ferry to meet our guides the fun of shopping was gone and the reality was setting in. There were no stores where we were going.

I patted her hand. She smiled again and looked stoically forward.

*What comforts are you willing to leave for adventure?
What comforts have you left for discovery?*

W.O.W: Wall of Water

At the orientation for the trip the guide said, "You will be cold, you will be hot. You will be wet or dry and you will suffer ..." I paid for this?

There were three phases to the Grand Canyon rafting trip. Phase 1 arrive safely. Phase II survive the rapids and camping for eight days and seven nights. Phase 3 return home safely. Without the pandemic my main fear would've been those rapids. I was surrounded by my friends, my wife and a guy I had known for 30 years who did the trip 10 years earlier. I was feeling good about the rapids until W.O.W. hit us - the wall of water.

In a perfect world, which never existed, there would've been beginner rapids to increase your confidence that you could handle the trip. But really, all you do is hold on, right? That's what you're thinking, you just hold on as you go through the rapids.

"This is a trip of extremes," the lead guide said as we went through orientation at Lee's Ferry which was the starting point. "You will be cold, you will be hot. You will be wet or dry and you will suffer. . And, you'll see amazing things." I don't recall any vacation with that type of introduction. We had our temperature taken when we signed in. As we packed we stepped into the cold water to cool our bodies and then we climbed onto the raft and launched our vacation. I took a seat behind Ed, the guy who had done the trip before. He sat bravely in the front seat on the left-side of the raft.

There were two rafts each 35-foot-long. Our entire group of 10 fit comfortably on one raft with usually five on each side. The other raft had 9 people and we motored along easily with a 30-horsepower motor. We danced through a few rapids that were mild but we hung on to a strap that secured the gear in the middle and a piece of rope that came up from the bottom between our legs. Our feet would rest on the raft's pontoon tubes as a third point of contact.

We would go over two hundred miles down the Colorado River. Water at the beginning of the trip was pulled from the bottom of the Glen Canyon dam and the temperature was close to 50°. It was cold but the air temperature was probably 90+. Our rain gear was close in our day bags but not on us. I knew there was something different coming when the assistant, a petite young woman who looked 15, came around the raft checking our grips.

"A big rapid coming, hold on," we were warned. I managed to slide slightly behind Ed to prevent getting drenched from the other rapids. If I turned slightly and I tucked behind him he bore the brunt of the water that splashed up on us. But, there was no hiding from the W.O.W., the wall of water. Time really does slow down in a moment like this.

The water was rough and we were getting a little wet when suddenly the nose of the boat teetered on the edge of an abyss. Is the hole there or does the water slip away? We hung suspended there for a long time, but you know it was maybe two seconds. We dropped and kept dropping into a hole defined by a wall of water ... I remember space; I remember the wall of water building in front of us, then above us and even higher above us. There was no splash of water. Just this wall of water that stood above the rim of the hole suspended in air is if waiting for us to arrive at the perfect spot. It held back all of the splashes of water that really wanted to get to us as if to say to them "Not yet, just wait." The wall had momentum and I gave it a personality. It was going to hit us full force and then stay in my mind's eye forever.

I yelled Chelsea's name because the wave would hit her too and for a nanosecond I believed she would be swept off the back of the boat. The boat dropped, but we (the passengers) stayed suspended momentarily until the ropes we held went with the raft, and then the thunderous wall of water hit us full force. There was no protection from someone else. It was like doing a vertical belly flop. Two opposing forces collided in midair. We all did a full frontal into the wall of water. We were flattened and Ed was shoved against me by the force created as the wall of water went through us one way and the boat pulled us downward then forward.

My hand stayed wrapped on the strap but my body was someplace else. The flexibility in my hand was used to the max. My hand collapsed and I had a moment wondering if I'd broken it. We came out the other side of the rapid sputtering, gasping checking ourselves and each other. Was my hand in one piece? Was my wife there? Was everyone in the boat? Yes to all questions.

"Did you see that wall of water?" I asked the kid on the other side of the boat. "It had to be 15 feet high!" He sputtered in response.

"Are you okay" I asked Ed and he responded. "Yeah, are you?" I looked at him again 10-15 seconds later. "You lost one of your glass lenses." It was true one of the lenses was completely gone from his glasses. We were both shook from the experience and shaking from the cold. We retreated to the back of the boat.

I turned to the guide. "I was holding onto the strap with my right hand and then the rope at my feet. I felt myself being swept away. What else could I do?"

"Use your other hand to hold onto another strap," he said quickly. My mind wasn't working well. I tried to apply what he said. I have one hand on the one strap and the other on the other rope, and he wanted me to use my third hand? The guy smiled as he saw my mind working to make sense of his recommendation. He was amused, I was not, but I didn't know him well enough to reprimand him or express my anger. Instead I asked.

"Do we have a lot of rapids like that?"

"You paid for white water rafting," he said easily and I anticipate he's said that many times, especially on the first day. I wanted to dislike him but he held my life in his hands. And, it's hard to argue with someone who is stating the obvious. He was right. I paid for this. The fears about getting there in the midst of a pandemic were replaced with the reality that I was really white water rafting. I needed a new strategy but there was only one reality.

There was only one way out of the canyon and that was via the river and through the rapids - a 270 mile trek downstream and seven nights of sleeping under the stars.

I go back to the guide's introduction, "You will be very cold, you will be very hot. You will be wet or dry, and you will suffer..." What would we have done with an introduction about the realities of 2020? Imagine a guide saying, " In the new year you will be tested as you've never been tested before. Healthcare will be pushed like it's never been pushed before in peace time. Protests will become a regular part of the news. Life as you know it will never be quite the same." What would we have done? Would we have believed it and if we did – would we have gotten out of bed to face a new day?

I think it's better when the guide says, "Hold on!" I don't need to know the other things. Life is like a river – there is quiet and there are rapids. Enjoy the quiet, be with friends, hold on in the rapids, push through the WOW's – the walls of water that wash through us, and know that we were meant to do this journey.

I paid for this? What do you wish you hadn't done? What do you wish you HAD done?

CAMPING 101

What do you need to learn today?

Repetition was needed. When we loaded the rafts at Lee's Ferry we loaded them using the bucket brigade of passing all the equipment from one person to the other, and then the guides secured the raft. When we arrived at our first night's camp, we were told the same thing.

"Bucket brigade to unload the rafts, but first go find your spot where you want to camp for the night. Drop your day bags and preservers and come back so we can unload the rafts. Then we'll demonstrate setting up cots and tents."

We followed Ed since he was our expert to find a place for the night. The 10 of us ended up being in a line with our feet facing the river. The cots were all in row forming a temporary military bunkhouse.

A bucket brigade was an all-hands-on-deck and one of the requirements of the trip. You had to be able to assist with unloading the rafts. We would form a line off the back of the raft and supplies were passed from person to person to form piles for kitchen supplies, temporary bathroom materials, cots, chairs, and personal bags. Many hands do make light work but a few of the bags were heavy which would become a form of public shaming. "Here comes bag 23," people would call out as the heaviest bag of all was passed from person to person. I was relieved to know bag 11 was not on that list, although my bag was not light either. We were all assigned a bag number which corresponded to our life preservers and instructed to grab a cot and a camp chair to take back to our newly created campsite.

On this first night Freddy led the tutorial of camp setup. As we gathered around him, the river providing the backdrop of noise, he began. "Each night you'll grab your bag, a cot and a chair to take to your site. In your bag there's a sleeping bag, a sheet and a tarp. The sheet is ideal to cover up with because many nights you won't need your sleeping bag. The temperature will be too hot. Some people even wet down their sheet to help cool them down. The tarp can be used to place under your cot to reduce the amount of sand that gets into your bag and if it rains you can throw the tarp over you to keep you dry."

"What about the tents?" someone asked.

"We have tents but the inside temperature of a tent is 15 degrees higher than outside. I doubt you'll need a tent," Freddy said.

Before arriving, I had every intention of having a tent. I wanted to take full advantage of whatever my 18 months of payments had secured for me after all - where would I change my clothes? But once I arrived, I never used a tent the entire time and had plenty of privacy for the few changes of clothes that I did. By the end I wasn't even changing clothes.

Freddy shook the cot out of its bag which was a similar size bag as a camp chair. He shook out the pieces and began assembling them by extending the mesh cot to its full height in front of him. "You'll need to extend the cot and then shake it to allow the side rails to fall. Feel for the pieces to interlock - they connect like a male and female piece together." He shook it out easily, adjusted it slightly and the two pieces locked together easily forming two solid side rails. He reached for the support pieces that would be the legs for the cot.

Jaimie from our group raised her hand slightly. "Do you have a diagram of those interlocking pieces? she asked. "Since we have a few lesbians here we might need to have that visual."

Jaime with her perfect delivery, a hint of devilry in her eye and a slight smile as an invitation for him to engage tossed out her question. Freddy was caught off guard.

"Just saying," Jaime added and a few of the people in our group chuckled a little letting him know this was not intended to place him on the defensive. Funny how you know that just by a few little sounds and comments.

His initial openness to answering questions and listening stumbled just for a moment. He recovered as soon as he saw her smile. He walked over gave her a high five and the rest of the group laughed too.

Later one of the campers told me when Jaimie made her comment, he knew we would be all right which made me realize how the others were seeing us. Even on vacation we are continually assessing to determine: Are you like me or not like me? Are you part of my tribe or not?

Jaimie's little quip called out the elephant in the room. There were six women or three couples who were not like the other 17 people on the trip but we had no intention to build walls and separate ourselves. Humor is a powerful thing and allows a mirror to be held up so we can see ourselves from a different view without always having to make demands to fit or be accepted. Sometimes we can all just 'be' and be okay with the differences and instead focus on the similarities. After all we were all making our way through an incredible experience – a trip of a lifetime.

The last detail where we needed assurance was regarding the toilet at the campsite. "As soon as we can, we will set up the toilet," Freddy explained. "We call it the Groover and we place it in a concealed area with a path leading to it. At the head of the trail there will be a hand washing station with two buckets – one holds clean water, the other holds gray water. A foot-pump moves the water to the faucet and soap is there to use. Please wash your hands frequently and then air dry them." He held up a Tupperware container filled with toilet paper and a red lid that read 'bathroom key'.

"This is how you know someone is at the groover. If this is gone someone is there – don't forget to bring it back! We've had people leave it and then have a line of campers waiting to go and they can't. Make sure you bring back the key!"

There was chuckling and shuffling of feet in the sand as he reviewed the bathroom details. Funny how obsessed we were with where we would 'go' and the detail he needed to go into, but he had a captive audience. He had answered all of these questions in the past so he knew what to share.

"And, the last thing we do before we get on the rafts in the morning is load the Groover. You'll have plenty of time to get coffee in the morning, do your business and pack for the day." He really did know our concerns.

Our very first night as Chelsea and I sat on our cots and dug through our main bag to find what we needed for the evening, we came to the same conclusion. We brought too much. We followed the packing guidelines they gave us, but slowly added a few extra batteries, another headlamp, another shirt, and other items ideal to survive in the hot canyon. We had bags within bags to make it easier to find things but our system wasn't working for us.

To really prepare for an overnight trip in the Grand Canyon you need to pack in advance weeks before you leave. We call this 'practice- pack'. The week before we leave, we pack and include everything we want. Once we see how outrageous our initial selection is we narrow down what we really take. But the Canyon trip needed one other element. We needed to pack and then place ourselves in a dark room with our bag and try to find the five things we needed to go to bed or for getting up in the middle of the night with only a headlamp. The goal is to do this without opening and closing every sub bag or without emptying all the contents on the cot or sleeping bag.

Make it a little contest – GO! Find the headlamp. Find the toothbrush and toothpaste. Where's a sleep shirt? What about camp footwear? What about the cooling towel for the hot nights or the extra-long sleeve shirt or pants for the cool morning? Can you organize yourself so that everything can be found within a minute? This is a great exercise and one I wish we had done prior to leaving our house and stepping onto the plane. It's all designed to reduce stress. However, it also reduces the entertainment for the rest of the campers.

I found out later that our fellow campers used Chelsea and I as their evening entertainment. They would get ready in the daylight and then sit back and watch the show. As much as we would try to get ready in the daylight, we always seemed to miss something. They'd watch us plow through our bags, unzipping and zipping little bags, as we tried to prepare ourselves for the evening. Or, as we tried to find the one thing we had forgotten to secure. We tried to be quiet but intense whispers really travel when there's no other sounds to block the noise.

I'm glad we entertained others, and I'm sure the true appreciation came from seeing their past selves in our angst. I'll enjoy it in the future when I watch others struggle.

What do you need to learn today and why is it important?

Vacation chores

Do you have goals on vacation? Things you really want to do and achieve when you venture from home? I had one...

Meditation is part of my daily routine and I thought meditating by the Colorado River in the middle of the Grand Canyon would be another way to connect and experience the canyon. At a resilience presentation the facilitator talked about having experiences of awe. She shared a picture of the Grand Canyon and explained the value of letting go and being in the moment and creating the memory in our mind's eye because the recall of that memory could bring calm and presence. Meditating would make me feel even more present as I experienced the Canyon for a week with no access to phone, internet, or anything else.

My meditation ritual is 20 minutes and concludes with daily readings from two books: "Pocketful of Miracles" by Joan Borysenko, PH.D. and "The Spontaneous Fulfillment of Desire" by Deepak Chopra. Each book I've had for a couple years.

The book with a daily meditation has a reading and prayer. This is my second full year of going through this book. I'm amazed at all I don't recall from the previous year and how much is striking me completely different than the past. I noticed this especially in April right after the COVID-19 challenges were becoming more real in Ohio and across our nation. Last year I underlined passages and this year I began to write the year next to each new underlined sentence. The year 2020 needs no other note. The year will stand alone on a global basis for its impact. And that's why I opted to take the physical book with me so I could continue my notations.

The other book 'Spontaneous Fulfillment of Desire' by Deepak Chopra's has seven principles one for each day of the week. Each has a chapter and ends with statements of how that principle can be further understood. I started using those in April and each day found them valuable to review and a great way to begin every day. I imagined how those words might strike me in a different way in nature and being with my lifelong friends.

The first morning I went down to the river around 5 AM with my two books and my life preserver to use as a cushion. Since I was still on east coast time I wasn't surprised I was awake. I set my watch for 20 minutes, settled in and smiled as I relaxed into the moment. I was in the Grand Canyon. I was sitting by the river and I allowed all the sounds to go through me as I went deeper into the moment. I heard noises that were close and then noises far away. The river moved past me, water moved over rocks, water lapped at the banks. People in the camp area rustled and moved, waking to the first morning. I heard sounds of a morning in nature. All felt right.

At the end of the meditation from the other side of the camp which was the furthest distance from me, the young assistant called out in a sing-song voice as if she was the keeper of the canyon and introducing us to it for the very time. "Good morning and welcome to Grand Canyon National Park," she dragged out that last part as if she was sweeping her arm across the Canyon walls. Then she ended her morning welcome with the most important fanfare, "Your coffee is ready." Her joy of being able to welcome us to our first morning in the canyon came through.

I smiled a whole body smile of gratitude and peace. Meditating in the Grand Canyon couldn't get much better than this. I felt as if I received a full body hug from the Canyon.

As I write this the memory of that moment centers me, quiets me and helps me connect to that essential moment of being present in the canyon. I am home and there is no one to wake me with a full fanfare like this, so I create it for myself.

Now when I wake up, I say to my two dogs stretched out on the bed, "Good Morning Angels!" And I love the fact that I am welcoming other beings at the same time.

Do you have goals on vacation? Things you really want to do and achieve when you venture from home? What will they be in the future?

_____
_____
_____
_____
_____
_____
_____
_____
_____
_____
_____
_____
_____
_____
_____
_____
_____
_____
_____
_____
_____
_____
_____
_____
_____

Coffee & Laughter

How do you get through a tough day? Try this approach ...

Day 1 was the WOW – Wall of Water. Day 2 was calmer with beautiful scenery, hikes to side canyons and the reassurance from the Lead Guide that the day was an easy one. Day 3, which would have more rapids like we faced in the beginning that would literally rock our boat, seemed far into the future. None of us had forgotten about the major rapids, but we compartmentalized the pending doom nicely. We were all worried and spoke about the rapids only in low voices, an afterthought to a regular conversation and resigned to the realization that there was only one way out of the canyon – through the rapids. There really was comfort in knowing that we are all in this boat together. Commonality builds connection. Why weren't we seeing more connection on the home front as we all faced COVID-19?

Day 3 I awoke and once I realized where I was the apprehension for what we faced settled in quickly. I inhaled deeply and was a bit disappointed that my inhale caught for a moment in my throat. Was that a bit of a sob? A little emotion remained from Day 1 and the Wall of Water. I was impacted even more than I realized. I said a small prayer for safety, asked for the courage to face the rapids and let the universe know any divine intervention given would be appreciated. The wall of water hung over my head like a tsunami waiting to break, but I was cheered by the idea of something small. Floating in one of the side bags was a small can of ice coffee that allowed me to focus on a small treat. Funny, I could feel the tsunami retreat, as if to say, "Coffee? Sounds good!" I headed to the raft to see if my small treat was still there.

At home I make my coffee the night before using a French press. I would make the coffee, filter and drain it before refrigerating it for the night. The morning indulgence was coffee poured over ice in my sippy cup along with a banana for breakfast. For a few years I had made time to go through a McDonalds drive through for an iced coffee with vanilla until they increased the price to $1.50. I'm too cheap to pay $.50 more for coffee. At one of our stops before arriving at Lees Ferry where the trip began, we purchased a few cans of Starbucks nitro coffee. One of my fellow travelers had said it was a good investment to have a couple cans with us. The temperature was going to be 100 plus degrees in the canyon – when we left civilization, I knew I was saying goodbye to iced coffee for a while.

Despite that I joked about wanting iced coffee on the first morning, and Denny (not his real name), the quiet guide, took me seriously. "We can get that for you." And he started to move earnestly in some direction.

"No I was joking," I assured him thinking it was a joke to have ice in the middle of a heat wave. Was that possible? But the morning of the rough rapids I remembered the can of coffee. One request and there it was in my hand. Beaten up and looking a little worse for wear but I had a can of iced coffee that had been hanging out in a bag on the side of a raft. The contents fizzed when opened due to nitro and felt wonderful going down. Step one to tackling a day of rapids – iced coffee. What else could I do?

I knew the rapids were going to be more intense so what was going to help? Well, this time we had our water pants and jackets. I went to the back of the boat with Chelsea and grabbed a seat near the snack bin. Being near chocolate would help me and doling out snacks to others might take my mind off of the treacherous waters. I held Chelsea's hand when I could which was definitely not during the rapids and I nearly sat on top of her. I should have had more faith that my little prayer would be answered, but apprehension doesn't help the mind operate clearly. There was something else that would help.

Laughter - specifically Jillian's laughter would lighten the experience. Jillian was there with her wife, her brother-in-law (BIL) and his son. I've known Jillian since her first day as a college freshman and through the years I've grown to appreciate her laughter more. Have you noticed that with any of your friends? There are a few people that have a laugh that erupts from them that is natural, spontaneous and infectious. Something delights and amuses them and their ability to express it opens the way for others to enjoy the experience too. There are also times that you laugh and you cannot stop yourself.

On this day the BIL and his 19-year-old son bravely sat in the front right seats of the raft. Any front seat caused you to get drenched and as we went through the week, we realized the guide seemed to be able to put certain people in more precarious spots, or was that just paranoia? And, we certainly did not know that on day 3 of the trip. As we rose and dropped through the rapids the two guys were slammed by wave after wave but who could predict the buffer that laughter would provide as well as the memory?

A wave would hit them, they would cry out as the shock of the cold water hit their faces "Oh right down my neck!"

Jillian chuckled the first time they cried out. "Oh, you big babies," her wife cried out to her brother. Sibling relationships are fascinating especially as adults with no parent around – this is where the real substance is revealed. I think this was the power of the TV show Friends – Monica and Ross's sibling relationship grounded the whole group with a relationship that would be tested, tried, but always rise above any challenge the group had. The sister calling them 'big babies' from the safety of the back of the boat – opened a door for a little bit of humor. Jillian indirectly felt supported to enjoy what was happening.

One of the guys cried out and the chuckle became laughter. Another wave hit them, another yell from them, and she laughed harder. Another wave sideswiped them and her laughter would go to another level. We all laughed along with Jillian and then laughed at Jillian's joy. Then the rapid ended. We hit calm water and we all settled back into our pre-rapid seats. Jillian was still chuckling as she played the scene over in her mind and then laugh out-loud at the memory, and then harder until she was wiping tears from her eyes. She was at that point where you know you should stop laughing, but now you laugh at your own laughter and you can't stop. And the laughter feels so good and you can't remember when you laughed this hard and you laugh even more. Then you feel the detox and you realize how much you needed that laughter.

We laughed with Jillian at the guys, then we laughed as Jillian remembered, and then we laughed at Jillian. How long has it been since you laughed like that?

Here's an idea for you. If you can, pick up your phone and call the person you shared that experience of detoxifying laughter. Start the call with "Remember when." And then go into details and see if some of the magic from that moment returns. You never know - your phone call may be exactly what the two of you need today. If you can't talk to that person, call the person who would appreciate knowing that story. Bring light and air to the memory - enjoy it again. Cement it into your DNA.

And, that's how I endured the second major day of rapids iced-coffee and Jillian's laughter.

How do you get through a tough day? When did you last laugh so hard you cried?

"Hey you guys...!"

How do you pause and savor the moment with friends?

Mornings in the canyon were stunning. We would be on the water sometimes as early as 7:30 but no later than 9:00. A hot breakfast and coffee greeted us as we awoke in the morning light. Camp was broken down, the rafts were loaded and we pushed off from the shore of the old campsite. The canyon walls greeted us with their stoic humility and beauty, blue sky formed the back drop to every picture, the sun would rise in the sky, and cooler temps would surround us.

We settled on the raft and made our way down the river. Collectively there'd be a momentary pause when we realized where we were. Jaimie, my friend of many adventures, would proclaim loudly as if shouting to someone other than the other 11 of us on the raft "Hey you guys, look where we are!" She lifted her arms as if embracing the entire scene around us and for a moment we were a raft in a sun-globe, not a snow globe, but a sun globe. Like an ornament hanging from a curved hook, we were a raft dangling from a wire placed in the water and then steeped into the experience like a teabag. The shaking of the sun globe was the little kid shaking us as we went through the rapids. But, for now, the scene was quiet except for the proclamation, "Hey you guys, look where we are ... "

We all yelled and shouted in agreement and then silence descended on us again and only the sound of the motor could be heard. Can you imagine greeting each day of your vacation like that "Hey you guys look where we are!"

Better yet imagine greeting each and every day with that type of excitement and fervor. Greeting the pending hours with eyes eager to see around every corner and taking in the vistas and the beauty of your surroundings. Imagine being deeply grateful where you are every day.

We certainly had reason to feel that way. We were living in the midst of one of the natural wonders of the world. We were surrounded by friends and in some cases family. We had plenty of food and people to prepare it for us. We had experts and guides to help us navigate the rapids and increase the experience through their knowledge of the canyon

If you use Maslow's theory as the model, we were hitting a lot of the levels out of the park. We had our basic needs met with food and shelter, safety due to the guides, belonging with friends and family. Did we achieve self-actualization? We might have had glimpses. How great if we could feel that way every day?

I haven't been around many people since that trip in August. COVID-19 is worse and there's a vaccine beginning to be rolled out. I sequester, but indulge briefly in images of being with my family gathered at my parents' home, my childhood home, once we are finally free of the pandemic. As I greet my siblings and their children, I will grab them and hold each one tight. Maybe even to the point that they laugh and tell me 'All right, all right – I'll be here for a few days!" But I won't let them go.

I imagine we are all together and there is a momentary lull and I can say, "Hey you guys, look where we are!" We will look around amazed. Tears might well in a few people's eyes, others will swallow the lump in their throat. If the moment gets too heavy someone will intervene, "Let's celebrate!" or "Raise a glass!" We are finally able to get together.

I imagine asking questions of one of those magical 20-something nieces or nephews, "Now that you've survived a pandemic what are you planning on doing now?" Their response will be animated and eager, "I plan to ..." And, they'll launch into step 1, step 2 or maybe even jump to step 5. Maybe they'll say, "The most important thing I want to do this and I want to finally get back to this ... "

At some point in the conversation, I will just fall into the moment and observe the connection from another point of view. I will see that magical person for the incredible being that they are and enjoy being in their presence. I'm listening, but hearing something else. I'll be caught in the excitement as if I'm caught in a rapid. I'm hearing their dreams, drinking in their vitality, and knowing they are more amazing than they ever knew before they endured a pandemic. I'll be there but not really listening. I'll be more attuned to the feeling. I am there in the grandeur of a relationship that had to be navigated from a distance. I feel like a canyon separated us and now the bridge has been built. And for the ones who shrug their shoulders to say, "My life isn't that much different now." I'll smile because they are just at the beginning and not seeing the wonder around them – their potential dazzles everyone but them.

New babies are being born in the family – born in the midst of this pandemic. I will go to their baptism and have another chance to say, "Hey you guys, look where we are!"

We will shake our heads in amazement and gaze at a new born like we've never seen a baby before. Well, we've never seen this one before. Their parents might complain that their baby is awake at night but this is another thing that will pass – another rapid before the next calm. I know they will get through and come out the other side.

There will be a new gratitude for the simple things in life. Being in a room with friends and family will be magic. A concert will be a bigger event than ever before. Eating in a restaurant without fear of being exposed will be a relaxing treat.

"Hey you guys, look where we are," will celebrate the moment and be a jumping off point for so much more. This is the new platform for unity, equality and seeing the world through new eyes.

How do you pause and savor the moment with friends?

Who Do You Take on Vacation?

I was not alone ...

Did you ever notice how many people you take with you on vacation for no extra cost? Family and friends come to mind as you move through your vacation days. It happens during regular days too, but those thoughts become part of the daily blur of our lives. Vacation makes way for new sights and sounds, new connections.

We noticed this on vacation when we saw something that reminded us of someone and say, "Oh, they would love that." And for a moment that person would be with us on our vacation as we reminisced.

In the Canyon as I crawled out of my cot in the morning and willed my back to straighten and then sustain my uneasy steps in deep sand, I thought of my older brother and thought, "Thank goodness he didn't come. His back pain would have never stood the morning ritual I am learning to adopt."

Here in the Canyon, one mile below the surface, there were even more people with me. The beauty of the canyon would fill all my senses with color, smell and sound and silence me as I drank everything into my cells. I would take a moment to capture the memory almost as a photograph and be very present. I was in awe. Then I would think of who else needed to see this with me. The answer was - everyone who works in healthcare battling COVID-19.

Remember that little catch in my throat the morning of facing the big rapids? The little sound that was almost a sob as I woke up and realized I might face another 'Wall of Water'? I believe that on a much bigger scale that's the same emotion that nurses, doctors and support staff have as they wake up to face COVID-19 every day. As I walked in the beauty of the Canyon I thought of their eyes above their masks, their chaffed faces from the protective gear, the weariness as they walked into the hospital to begin a shift, or the weariness when they left and climbed into their car. All of those people were with me. As much as I wanted to be in the moment and on vacation, all of them were with me. Somehow, I wanted them to be healed, or at least to have the resources so they could keep going even though we had no idea how long the COVID-19 fight would be. The beauty in nature helps people heal.

Back in the real world, experts claimed healthcare workers could experience PTSD (Post Traumatic Stress Disorder) after COVID-19 ended. That comment really got my attention. The reality of PTSD hit me when a summer fireworks display sent a military family member launching out of bed and hitting the ground to take cover. Knowing about PTSD and having a family member react in that fashion changed PTSD for me.

Our minds are funny things and wonderful tools. How we use it to survive and cope is admirable, but where is the breaking point and how long could healthcare workers keep doing this work especially since they were burned out before COVID-19 hit.

I respected the work of the medical staff and what they did on a daily basis prior to COVID-19. But when COVID-19 happened my admiration for our healthcare team increased exponentially. Each day they ventured into the hospitals and in some cases people's homes due to our home care services. Early on they had no idea what they were facing or what they were exposing their families to in the process. Our daily dashboards shared the metrics of impact including the number of our associates quarantined due to exposure.

All of this was in the back of my mind as I walked through the canyon and an innocent discussion would bring work back to me in a moment.

"Do you take private groups down the river or just public groups?" I asked one of the young guides one day as we hiked along one of the side canyons.

"Both and the private groups are very interesting," she said. "We've taken religious groups, and veterans with PTSD." A seed was planted with that conversation. If veterans were taken down the canyon to help them cope with PTSD, why couldn't healthcare workers do the same?

I heard of soldiers returning state side after being in combat attending sessions where they explored questions like: What did I learn? How will this experience make me a better spouse, parent, friend, or relative? Imagine - healthcare workers who could finally take a break, leave the bedside to enter the canyon and process what they endured.

Space was needed after the frenetic and overloaded pace of COVID-19 for people to just be and not jump to the next fire. They needed to decompress and not just for an evening, or even a weekend. They needed space to let go and drop below to explore another level and release, and then move to another level, explore and release again. Space was there in the canyon and levels would open up as the days went past.

They would never forget the patient's hands they held as the patient left this world and passed on. They would never forget the families they spoke to as they shared good and bad news. Could they ever be free of the weight they carried shift after shift, month after month, 2020 into 2021? Forgetting is an option, but not recommended. Finding meaning in the experience and learning from the time was one step in the healing process. There would be many steps in the process. Finding space and being in nature was one path.

I would have moments of bliss in the canyon and then in a heartbeat wish that my moments could be shared with my colleagues at the front lines of COVID-19. They were with me every day.

For your next vacation – who do you want to take with you and why? BTW – You don't have to limit yourself to reality.

Why We Do What We Do

Who is the most important person to please...

Why do we do what we do? And when does the reason matter? There were a couple of tough hikes and daring things to do in the course of the trip and there were times that I sat out with no regrets. There were other times I opted in with regrets. Shouldn't that be the other way around?

The main canyon and the Colorado River are filled by countless side streams from side canyons. We hiked one or two every day of the trip, but this particular day there were options. You could choose to hike to another area that had a beautiful view and small oasis or stay close to the river and bath and lounge near another waterfall. I loved the idea of the hike but didn't realize it was going to be a stressful adventure. There were clues that Chelsea and I shouldn't have joined in.

For example, when I asked the trip guide how long the hike was to get an idea of how strenuous it was he hesitated and then moved his hand back-and-forth to form a 'Z' in the air.

"Oh," I said. "It's a zigzag."

He hesitated a little, "Yes, yes a zigzag."

We've done a number of strenuous hikes that were zigzags to help navigate steep areas, but this was not exactly a zigzag. No, not at all.

The other raft arrived before us and a few people stayed behind. "I don't have anything to prove," the one guy said. "I'll just stay here and relax." I thought about his comment a lot later on – he had nothing to prove. Did I?

The next clue was when we went to change from our water sandals into our hiking shoes. We followed the path to find the people from the other raft sitting above us on the edge of the cliff looking like small mountain goats perched among the rocks changing their shoes. The path to their perch went straight up a rock face and the fact that there were two or three 70 years old up there was the main reason I thought 'I can do this.'

Plus, I couldn't imagine that the rest of the hike was going to be straight up the cliff like that but I should've asked. Later Chelsea would tell me she thought the same thing. Maybe our final clue was when someone in our group turned back and said he couldn't take it anymore but Chelsea and I kept going. I kept going because of those 70 years old in front of me. They were making their way through this fairly easily and I just couldn't believe I couldn't do it if a 70-year-old was picking their way up the side of this rock face.

What I realize now was that the path wasn't a zigzag unless you consider going straight up a zigzag. There were a few steps that would be flat and the path would venture to the right or left, but then the climb would go straight up again with a careful review to find footholds and handholds to move to the next level. The grips were not always easy to find and I clung in place a few times either waiting for the person ahead of me or trying to decipher my own path. During those times I had momentary lapses into fear as I wondered how I was going to go back down since usually climbing down is much harder than going up. And that thought kept returning to me time and time again as I tried to find the right spot to place my hand and then my foot. As I made my way up those ledges I kept thinking, "Coming down is going to be horrible."

It was as if there was a little angel perched on my right shoulder, and there was a devil on my left shoulder. The angel on the right was encouraging saying, "We can do this! Imagine how beautiful it will look at the top." If I slipped the angel would say, "Good catch you're doing great!" But I could imagine the angel might look at the devil with wide eyes as if to say 'we're screwed'.

On the left the devil said, "Yeah you can do this – if a seventy-year-old woman and man can do this climb so can we! We will not be shamed by being out climbed!" My she-devil fumed with frustration when I didn't go faster and shook her fist at the rocks

I noticed the angel kept her perspective focused on the positive of what was going to be acquired or experienced while the devil was more about comparison. We shouldn't compare but sometimes it's a good fuel for the fire, but we shouldn't really compare. Bad devil, but aren't they always bad?

So as I continued up the mountain hand over hand placing one hand carefully, grip the rock and then move my foot into place. Then the second hand carefully moved, then the second foot and then we would get to a ridge to be able to walk five steps 1,2,3,4,5 and then do the same thing tediously again. Hand over hand, step over step, to get to the next ridge and that's how the whole thing was a zigzag up. I kept wondering when this would end and as I climbed and the climb was harder the angels voice quieted, but the devils voice got louder.

"This is gonna suck coming down – don't you know it? It's harder coming down than it is going up."

"Be quiet," Angel said. "Let her concentrate."

"I'm just being real – it's going to be hard and it's getting hotter." Devil said. "When did she drink water last?"

When did I drink water last? I have to be hydrated – I thought to myself.

"You better drink," said Angel.

"Yeah, you better drink because it's going to be harder coming down. You think it's hard going up? It's going to be harder coming down." Devil always had to finish.

The conversation in my head was so real that now the two felt like flies around my head. I felt like I could swipe them away with a hand that was needed to cling to the mountain. That's when I knew I needed to get present and focus on the task at hand. Deep breathe. Place hand, place foot, be in the moment, keep going.

Just then one of the guys turned back. "I can't do it," he said. I considered going with him, but hesitating meant I was going to try to catch up to him. He was already out of my sight and I have no sense of direction. I had a brief vision of being lost in the Grand Canyon the way I get lost in a shopping mall. It was best to stay with the group. We finally made it to a resting place, not the oasis.

The views were amazing. The river looked like a creek from as high up as we were. I stayed safely away from the edge and sat down. I was terrified, shaking like a leaf probably looking 10 years older than I was. I drank from my water bottle doing a body scan to see if I was truly fine or just a basket case. You know the answer.

There was more to go and the guides stood there young and rested within 20 seconds, eager to go on but they were clear about the path. "There's no more climbing to get to the oasis area but it is a narrow path that requires you to face the rock wall, slide meticulously, and walk sideways as you inch along the cliff and there's a bad drop." I wish I could tell you that I faced my fear and decided to do the last part of the hike that was really the main reason for the hike – to see this oasis in the canyon. But that would not be the truth. I don't think Chelsea and I even looked at each other. "We're good – we will stay here and meet you back here."

One other person stayed back with us. This was the fifth day of the trip. I knew a sure way to calm myself would be to write, but I didn't want to be rude. We had no idea how long we would wait, but to entertain ourselves we discussed the food we had eaten to date and I recorded the details in my journal noting all the meals and desserts. Even a virtual cheesecake or chocolate cake calms the nerves. The rest of the group returned, assuring us they would share their pictures, but I also thought they looked a bit rattled. I made the right choice to sit and talk food, especially desserts.

The pictures from the height of our turning point look amazing. We are all smiling, arms wrapped around each other with a backdrop that still takes my breath away. Then we gathered our backpacks, water bottles and walking sticks and headed back. Guess what? No angels and devils having discussions in my ear. They might have been there but the angel won. The trip back was significantly better than I anticipated with one exception. Chelsea got caught into a crevice that made her look like she was an open pair of scissors that had forgotten to close before going back into the drawer. If it wasn't for Jillian below giving her some guidance, I think we might still be sitting there waiting for her to figure out how to get out of that predicament.

Freddy asked what we thought when we returned. I gave him a little bit of an attitude and not the joking kind that's easy to dismiss. I finally had to admit to myself that I didn't ask the right questions, but I wasn't trying to prove anything either. I was trying to get steps on my pedometer and see great views. Both goals I accomplished. But the adventures weren't done.

Toward the end of the trip there was the chance to jump off a cliff to the water 15 feet below. Chelsea and I offered to take photos and videos of people making the leap. The rest of the group was split – some dashed up to the launch point eager to jump off, others walked up tentatively, while others went up under the guise they would observe from the top.

Later Ed would say that jumping off was easy, getting back up was the hard part. There were two ways to get out of the water. One was to climb up the side of the cliff using a knotted rope. If there are grips for your feet that seems like a good option, but people said there were few places to grip, plus the shoes and rock were wet. Upper body strength was needed. The second was to swim back over to the boat which always seems innocent until you are half way between where you were and where you want to be. Distance in water is deceiving. My decision to take pics was a good one.

The guy who said he had nothing to prove for the hike was one of the first ones to jump off. I wondered later if this was a bucket list item for him. I counted my jumping off the high dive in college to become a lifeguard my leap. I had nothing to prove. Yet, sometimes a leap isn't about proving something. Sometimes it's about returning to a place you didn't know you left and it's been waiting for you.

We had a few younger women on the trip. My relationships with my friends are older than these women and I have to calculate to see where they are on their journey because age is elusive to me. One woman was divorced. A dear friend of mine says divorce and grief change your brain. Isn't that an interesting and disturbing reference? If that's true – imagine falling in love when you are in your 20's, having the big wedding, beginning your life together, and then falling out of love and starting over. How does your brain change in this situation? I imagine that the intuition that told you to leap into love is still there, but maybe you don't trust yourself as much to make decisions. Perhaps that leap into love was a leap of faith and sitting home, especially during a pandemic, makes you think once, twice and maybe more about what you've done in the past that brings you... here. I can only speculate.

One of those younger women after holding back and being quiet, jumped. First, she peered over the edge for a moment, then walked back and then boldly forward, grabbed the sides of her life preserver and jumped. My heart leapt as I saw her fly through the air. She resurfaced triumphant and later said, "I felt the old me coming back. I used to do stuff like that all the time."

She needed to make that leap, and then realized the one she needed to please was her old self, her true self. Did I see a little more swagger in her step as she came back to the raft? There's a great leap, leap to your true self.

How do you honor your true self?

Passion and synchronicity

I love to see people passionate about their job and I find synchronicity to be interesting. When those two things occur together life seems a little more fun.

People who are passionate about their jobs get everyone's attention. My interest is not just because I'm in Human Resources. If you love your job, you see a kindred spirit. If you hate your job, you see someone you desire to be. When you see them on vacation there's always an interesting back story. Perhaps seeing synchronicity in this setting is as natural as a raft moving down a river.

The Grand Canyon continued to unfold before us as our rafts either meandered through the calm spaces between or rushed through the rapids. The guides and assistants were amazing and the faith we placed in them was nothing short of putting our lives in their hands. During the day their hands were on the rudder of the engine that propelled us forward, or tucked us into an eddy for a brief break after running a rapid. They also found the space on the river's edge that opened up to side canyons and beautiful views that were a walk through either a dry creek bed or one that could be walked through easily with just water shoes.. At night they set up camp, a kitchen, a new groover (aka toilet in the world outside of the Grand Canyon) and then prepared an incredible meal for us.

Their knowledge ran the gamut of knowing each turn and drop of the river, the history of the canyon as well as the indigenous tribes. Their sense of humor managed 19 disparate characters living in a strange, but beautiful, environment. The guide joked on the first day that he felt like he was leading kindergartners who constantly asked, "What should I wear today?" Which stopped me from asking that question, but I wanted to know so much more. What was the worst situation they had ever handled, and then I didn't ask the question because did I really need to know that now? Had anyone ever died on the trip? Did I really want to know that answer? I kept a lot of questions to myself.

These people are passionate about their work and a big part is their love of the canyon. Even the one assistant who was only 21 had five years of experience on the river. She's been working since 16 and her guidebook had copious notes written into each page of the spiral bound maps so her history sessions to us were accurate and informative. The guides scan the sides of the canyon so they could point out big horn sheep, mule deer, heron, and condors. They also gave insight to the layers of rock and how the different stages of the canyon have been created. I would never remember the detail but the years and evolution amazed me. One guide showed how the river continues to change even visible in his lifetime. There'd been one beach the size of a football field ideal for a campsite that was gone due to erosion and ongoing changes. These people loved their job, but look at their office. They were in the majestic presence of the Grand Canyon.

Our second guide worked for the company for 16 years and was a manager in the warehouse. The rafting company runs full canyon trips that last from 7-15 days, plus 3-day trips from May-October. Imagine the logistics of transitioning supplies off the river, moving rafts, and restocking all the trips plus the challenge with the new COVID-19 protocols. He did a couple trips a year down the river just so he could be attune to the needs of the guests and guides. Nice little job perk floating down the river of the Grand Canyon, but remember he had to do so with 20 people like me asking tons of questions each day. But he didn't mind. He had also hiked endless miles, and backpacked into corners of the canyon. This beautiful place was his home. His biggest regret was that he couldn't share as much as he usually did.

"I normally read different passages and say more," he said. "But I'm losing my voice." Projecting his message to the front of the 35 foot raft was a challenge and there was much he wanted to share. Off to the side, he'd share things and people around him would share the details with the rest of the group. However, his passion was lost in translation.

We rotated guides and boats to give us variety and give them a break. It was probably day 6 so this was my third trip with Denny. The majestic walls were near us and there were more in the distance. The layering of one beyond the other provided depth, but the size was hard to comprehend. My mind played tricks on me as I saw patterns in the rocks and in the side of the walls. The first day I pointed out the picture of the painting 'The Last Supper" which I thought would be unique but the images kept coming. In the distance I could see buildings from Athens Greece, temples from the Acropolis, cathedrals from Europe, pillars like those in Mexico that I saw a year ago. My mind saw all of these and more. Was I losing my mind?

This was a question for DAY 6. A question to pose with just a slight amount of hesitancy so if someone looked at me oddly and said, "You're crazy." I could laugh it off.

"Do other people see cathedrals and temples?" I asked hesitantly and a little reverently. Awe is something anyone can appreciate.

He caught my eye, and there was that moment of a pause when you connect on a new level with someone. It's frequently caused by a shared vulnerability and I think I had just entered his sacred space. He smiled slightly; this was a man of few words. "Read what she's reading," he said. His assistant held a typed page in her hands and she read it quickly before handing it over to me.

I read ...

"I think my preconceived conception of the Cañon was the same conception most people have before they come to see it for themselves—a straight up-and-down slit in the earth, fabulously steep and fabulously deep; nevertheless merely a slit. It is no such thing.

Imagine, if you can, a monster of a hollow approximately some hundreds of miles long and a mile deep, and anywhere from ten to sixteen miles wide, with a mountain range—the most wonderful mountain range in the world—planted in it;

so that, viewing the spectacle from above, you get the illusion of being in a stationary airship, anchored up among the clouds; imagine these mountain peaks—hundreds upon hundreds of them—rising one behind the other, stretching away in endless, serried rank until the eye swims and the mind staggers at the task of trying to count them; imagine them splashed and splattered over with all the earthly colors you ever saw and a lot of unearthly colors you never saw before; imagine them carved and fretted and scrolled into all shapes—tabernacles, pyramids, battleships, obelisks, Moorish palaces—the Moorish suggestion is especially pronounced both in colorings and in shapes—monuments, minarets, temples, turrets, castles, spires, domes, tents, tepees, wigwams, shafts." [Pg 30]

I read those last few lines and my eyes opened wider, and I smiled a little more. What is the chance that I would ask about temples and churches at the exact moment he handed that typed page to his assistant? What is the chance that I would be on the same raft with him when he has that page out? This is synchronicity brought about by passion. Some people call synchronicity 'God winks' – it's the way the divine shows you are on the right path.

By the way this piece is from <u>Roughing it Deluxe</u> by Irvin S. Cobb and is in the section titled ' A Pilgrim

Canonized'. It was first published in 1913. And it was created just for my moment in the Grand Canyon. Well, that's what it felt like on that day.

There was one more little synchronicity when I returned home. I couldn't stop thinking about the canyon and the river. Essays filled my journal as ideas came to me. I was hesitant to share with others, but a friend told me, "You are given experiences so you can share with others." I turned to my office and put on my old ipod and the song 'The River' by Garth Brooks came on immediately. I smiled again. I think I've been summoned, not invited.

Where have you seen passion and synchronicity in your life? What was the impact of that discovery on you?

What Awakens You?

Do you realize how you sleep through your life ...

What awakens you? What's getting and keeping your attention in a positive way right now? Have you had to experience that changed you and impacted you in a fundamental way? One that stayed with you and won't let go of you? That's how the Grand Canyon rafting trip was for me and I found out later I wasn't alone.

I had the typical reentry challenges for vacation that I always had but here it was two weeks later and the experience continued to be with me. Little things made me smile and took me back to the essence of the trip just being in the moment. For resilience that's what they recommend. When you are caught in beauty or awe give into it completely and then make a memory. It could be the same as taking a mental photograph or allowing the sights, sounds, and the feelings to be cemented into your mind and your being.

Living on and in a river for eight days and seven nights awakened me. Rafting on the river, standing in the river, listening for the river – all of it changed my relationship and my experience with the idea of a river. It wasn't the same as being on a ship in the ocean. Were we feeling more because of COVID-19? Was the isolation of COVID-19, and not being able to return to other activities that could get us back into our real lives, making us feel more? Maybe real lives were too real and we wanted to keep the magic alive.

I asked the one guide if she noticed a difference with the groups so far this year. She thought about it but had not noticed anything in particular. I have a theory about COVID-19 that's stripping away so much of the armor that we have and now that it's removed we feel more and think deeper. Things resonate at a level we previously have opted to ignore.

I think the canyon holds all the mysteries and history of the world. In every side canyon there is the telling of part of our history but there's also etchings hidden in plain sight that tell the future. The challenge is our conscious mind can't discern the patterns of the future, or recognize them for what they are so we can only pull forward the wisdom once it reflects our experience.

This idea came to me because of some graffiti I saw on the canyon walls, or at least that's what I thought I was seeing. In large black block letters chiseled in brown stone was the word IPAD. The letters were close together and best distinguished from a distance. I shook my head disappointed to see the words written on the wall, and then surprised we hadn't seen any other graffiti. But, as I drew closer I realized the image wasn't graffiti at all just my mind making sense of the configurations of the rock revealing a word to me that wasn't really there.

Being in the Canyon can make you feel insignificant, just like COVID-19. You can feel like a grain of sand with no significance. Our lives before COVID-19 could have been the lull of the motor taking us through our lives that really were extraordinary but we didn't know it then. Now COVID-19 is the rapids tossing us, shaking us from our slumber to challenge us to clarify what is important and where should we spend our time? How do we keep alive in us the things that are important to us? It's also telling us that we are significant and that each thing we do makes a difference, and an impact. That's the journey we are on – moving from insignificance to significance.

At work we talk about COVID Courage. This was a phrase coined over the summer when people went to outdoor parties and many people did not wear masks to events. We said 'COVID Courage' was being the one in the room who did wear a mask or the ones in the family who turned down family events to reduce the spread of the disease.

Then a friend told me her version of COVID Courage. She had been ill during COVID – not due to COVID-19, but for other reasons and had nearly died. She stays sequestered because her resistance is significantly compromised. In the last few months she has explored more of her creative side. She's featuring her creative work on a youtube channel to share her crafts and how she decorates. She's stopped listening to her internal critic who tells her she can't or shouldn't do things. "This is MY form of COVID Courage," she says. "I'm finally going to share my creative side with others and not allow myself to be held back any longer."

This is the next step of COVID Courage – exploring the things that have held us back before as well as exploring anything new that came to us in 2020 and beyond that holds us back. Being vigilant for over 12 months will leave a mark, unless we have the courage to explore it and realize we can learn and move forward. Each of us has a Grand Canyon within us waiting to be explored and awakened.

What is awakening you now in your life?

Endings

End to begin the next adventure...

Endings can be unifying, celebratory, reflective. There was an element of each in ours. At the beginning Guide Freddy said people could be on either raft and usually the rafts would merge and people would mix. Probably due to our group being together the rafts stayed separate but we grew to know each other as we hiked, ate together and gathered at night. On the last night the guides had some final words and we had a special song that we created and sang for them sung to the 12 days of Christmas as we reflected on the trip. .

The song was a neat little project prompting more connection but each day peeled the onion back of our lives a little more. Surface discussions prompted more questions and more discussions and we shared our stories. We could all write books of our lives and I welcomed the chance to do a deep dive with every person to hear what brought them to this point. Even the young people had already endured so much that it took my breath away to know of the illnesses their sibling faced and what the family survived together. More late nights and hikes (on flat ground) were needed to unpack all of it, but the eight day and seven nights ended with fanfare and much love.

The morning of the last day we ceremoniously lined the last 20 feet to the rafts and greeted the guide as they hauled in the groover or the toilet for the last time. They said "We aren't taking any more of your crap!" We all laughed. We were thrilled to see it go, amazed at the one part of our trip that caused anxiety and release was behind us. Denny and the assistant carried it as we sang the song from 'The Sound of Music':

> *"So long, Farewell*
> *Aufwiedersehn*
> *Adeiu, Adeiu Adeiu*
> *To yieu and yieu and yieu"*

Then we'd twirl, make weird 'doot, doot, and doodledoo' noises and launch into the song again. We were adults being weird, laughing, and loving the craziness of the moment. All done in the bright morning sun fueled by nothing more potent than coffee.

We floated down the river for an hour or so that last day and then unloaded, reduced the rafts from 2 to 1 by taking off the pontoons on the far sides and strapping them together. We floated further down to our extraction point merged as one laughing and eating our lunch passing around cookies and candy as if we were one family. We broke into the song once more and tried to hold onto the time together as the last of our trip floated by.

We would do the last 50 miles by a speed boat while the combined raft took eight hours to do the same stretch. We parted company with our guides at the speedboat. They knew that after our safety session we would catch up with them soon enough. The safety session was distracting as the group schemed of ways to say good-bye to our guides as we whipped past them. You can imagine the final decision. A handful of people dropped their pants to moon the guides as our final goodbye. I saw nothing except the shocked look of our guides as we sped past them. And then we settled back watching the rest of the canyon drift away and already started to turn our attention to a real shower, clean sheets, a real bed and maybe having pizza for dinner later on.

At the hotel I was moved to the front of the line for a shower – I anticipate not changing clothes for a few days was catching up to my travel mates. Pizza was wonderful and slipping between clean sheets was too delicious to fall asleep to – the sensation needed to be savored more, but sleep was its own reward.

Travel back home was uneventful for all of us and we were looking forward to Labor Day weekend when we would reconnect again. It's always helpful to have something to look forward to especially the next time we would see each other.

Jaimie and her wife have a wonderful property in the middle of nowhere or so it seems with acres of green grass, beautiful landscaping, and a pond bigger than my postage stamp property in the middle of town in another part of Ohio. When we arrived a few weeks later we hugged still wearing masks, and then trying to keep our distance.

Jaimie was bubbling as always a wide smile greeting all of us, "I love you guys. We missed you!" She would say 'missed' as if the word was coming out of a dog's squeak toy. Her voice would go up an octave and then drop down again. If I had thought of it, I would've realized she had a surprise.

On the second night of our weekend, she opened a package and pulled out a huge blower and a large piece of plastic compacted into a square. "It's an adult jumping pit," she said. I didn't say anything but I knew that there was not enough material to support any one of us, let alone two of us jumping in a pit. Eventually the form took shape and before us was a huge 20 foot white screen for us to project the pictures and videos from the trip. As nighttime came the screen went up and our technology person helped make each system talk to the projector. There we were on the big screen.

Imagine a dark summer evening sitting in Ohio watching your adventure from a month earlier on the big screen. We laughed as we heard our screams, our comments, and saw the beauty of the Canyon. We were speechless also and when it ended a few of us broke into tears.

"I can't believe we did it!"

"We did that!"

We shook our heads. What a great trip and the only way to take the risk was with people you love.

"What's next?" We asked each other. We were already planning the next adventure.

What is ending for you and what is beginning for you?

About the Author

Sue Hiser, your canyon tour guide in spirit, is the author of three books, executive & life coach, speaker, and facilitator. She is passionate about learning and helping people achieve their goals as they live their dreams. Along with reading and writing, she loves to travel. Originally from Upstate New York, she is married, has two dogs and lives in Columbus, Ohio.

As a coach in healthcare she is seeing first-hand the impact of COVID-19 on professionals, the system and the community. She hopes her experiences will encourage those impacted by the effects of the virus to keep moving forward in even the most difficult of times. One day, we will be able reflect on our experiences and say, "I can't believe we did it!"

For more information on Sue Hiser and her work, please visit www.suehiser.com.